Ephesians 5

By

Angel Perez Santiago
BTH, BCA, MA

Angel Perez Santiago

Angel was saved through the ministry of Teen Challenge in New York City. After being delivered from addiction, he attended Trinity Bible Institute in North Dakota where he met his wife Sandra. They are the parents of three children and six grandchildren with one on the way.

Angel holds several Bachelors' degrees and a Master of Arts in Pastoral Counseling. He has traveled around the world preaching and teaching the word of God. He has a great passion for missions and is involved in the feeding of many children in the Philippines. Angel gives pastoral oversight to many ministers in the Philippines and the USA

Welcome to these sermon notes in Ephesians 5. I trust that as we study together that we can grow in grace and in the Lord Jesus Christ. In this chapter Paul talks about practical issues that we face every day. May God bless you real good as you study God's word is my prayer for you. These sermon notes were developed for teaching and preaching to my congregation. They are expository in nature and easy to follow

Text for study
Ephesians 5

(Ephesians 5:1-33) Therefore be imitators of God as dear children. And walk in love, as Christ also has loved us and given Himself for us, an offering and a sacrifice to God for a sweet-smelling aroma. But fornication and all uncleanness or covetousness, let it not even be named among you, as is fitting for saints; neither filthiness, nor foolish talking, nor coarse jesting, which are not fitting, but rather giving of thanks. For this you know, that no fornicator, unclean person, nor covetous man, who is an idolater, has any inheritance in the kingdom of Christ and God. Let no one deceive you with empty words, for because of these things the wrath of God comes upon the sons of disobedience. Therefore do not be partakers with them. For you were once darkness, but now you are light in the Lord. Walk as children of light (for the fruit of the Spirit is in all goodness, righteousness, and truth), finding out what is acceptable to the Lord. And have no fellowship with the unfruitful works of darkness, but rather expose them. For it is shameful even to speak of those things which are done by them in secret. But all things that are exposed are made manifest by the light, for whatever makes manifest is light. Therefore He says: "Awake, you who sleep, Arise from the dead, And Christ will give you light." See then that you walk circumspectly, not as fools but as wise, redeeming the time, because the days are evil. Therefore do not be unwise, but understand what the will of the Lord is. And do not be drunk with wine, in which is dissipation; but be filled with the Spirit, speaking to one another in psalms and hymns and spiritual songs, singing and making melody in your heart to the Lord, giving thanks always for all things to God the Father in the name of our Lord Jesus Christ, submitting to one another in the fear of God. Wives, submit to your own husbands, as to the Lord. For the husband is head of the wife, as also Christ is head of the church; and He is the Savior of the body. Therefore, just as the church is subject to Christ, so let the wives be to their own husbands in everything. Husbands, love your wives, just as Christ also loved the church and gave Himself for her, that He might sanctify and cleanse her with the washing of water by the word, that He might present her to Himself a glorious church, not having spot or wrinkle or any such thing, but that she should be holy and without blemish. So husbands ought to love their own wives as their own bodies; he who loves his wife loves himself. For no one ever hated his own flesh, but nourishes and cherishes it, just as the Lord does the church. For we are members of His body, of His flesh and of His bones. "For this reason a man shall leave his father and mother and be joined to his wife, and the two shall become one flesh." This is a great mystery, but I speak concerning Christ and the church. Nevertheless let each one of you in particular so love his own wife as himself, and let the wife see that she respects her husband. (NKJV)

Ephesians 5:1-7

Ephesian 5:1 ¶ Be <ginomai> ye <mimetes> therefore <oun> **followers <mimetes>** of God, <theos> as <hos> **dear <agapetos> children; <teknon>** (KJV)

1 ¶ Therefore be imitators of God as dear children. (NKJV)

Key words

Followers, mimetes; an imitator:--follower

Dear, agapetos; beloved:--(dearly, well) beloved, dear.

Children, teknon; a child (as produced):--child, daughter, son.

Matthew 5:45 "that you may be sons of your Father in heaven; for He makes His sun rise on the evil and on the good, and sends rain on the just and on the unjust. (NKJV)

Matthew 5:48 "Therefore you shall be perfect, just as your Father in heaven is perfect. (NKJV)

Luke 6:36 "Therefore be merciful, just as your Father also is merciful. (NKJV)

Ephesians 4:32 And be kind to one another, tenderhearted, forgiving one another, just as God in Christ forgave you. (NKJV)

Ephesian 5:2 And <kai> *walk <peripateo>* in <en> *love, <agape>* as <kathos> Christ <Christos> also <kai> hath loved <agapao> us, <hemas> and <kai> hath *given <paradidomi>* himself <heautou> for <huper> us <hemon> an *offering <prosphora>* and <kai> a *sacrifice <thusia>* to God <theos> for <eis> a *sweetsmelling <euodia> savour.* <osme> (KJV)

2 And walk in love, as Christ also has loved us and given Himself for us, an offering and a sacrifice to God for a sweet-smelling aroma. (NKJV)

Key words

Walk, peripateo; to tread all around, i.e. walk at large (especially as proof of ability); figuratively, to live, deport oneself, follow (as a companion or votary):--go, be occupied with, walk (about).

Love, agape; love, i.e. affection or benevolence; specially (plural) a love-feast:--(feast of) charity(-ably), dear, love.

Given, paradidomi; to surrender, i.e yield up, intrust, transmit:--betray, bring forth, cast, commit, deliver (up), give (over, up), hazard, put in prison, recommend.

Offering, prosphora; presentation; concretely, an oblation (bloodless) or sacrifice:--offering (up).

Sacrifice, thusia; sacrifice (the act or the victim, literally or figuratively):--sacrifice.

Sweetsmelling, euodia; good-scentedness, i.e. fragrance:--sweet savour (smell, -smelling).

Savour, osme; fragrance (literally or figuratively):--odour, savour.

Genesis 8:21 And the LORD smelled a soothing aroma. Then the LORD said in His heart, "I will never again curse the ground for man's sake, although the imagination of man's heart is evil from his youth; nor will I again destroy every living thing as I have done. (NKJV)

Leviticus 1:9 'but he shall wash its entrails and its legs with water. And the priest shall burn all on the altar as a burnt sacrifice, an offering made by fire, a sweet aroma to the LORD. (NKJV)

John 13:34 "A new commandment I give to you, that you love one another; as I have loved you, that you also love one another. (NKJV)

John 15:12 "This is My commandment, that you love one another as I have loved you. (NKJV)

2 Corinthians 2:15 For we are to God the fragrance of Christ among those who are being saved and among those who are perishing. (NKJV)

Galatians 1:4 who gave Himself for our sins, that He might deliver us from this present evil age, according to the will of our God and Father, (NKJV)

Galatians 2:20 "I have been crucified with Christ; it is no longer I who live, but Christ lives in me; and the life which I now live in the flesh I live by faith in the Son of God, who loved me and gave Himself for me. (NKJV)

1 Thessalonians 4:9 But concerning brotherly love you have no need that I should write to you, for you yourselves are taught by God to love one another; (NKJV)

Hebrews 7:27 who does not need daily, as those high priests, to offer up sacrifices, first for His own sins and then for the people's, for this He did once for all when He offered up Himself. (NKJV)

Hebrews 9:14 how much more shall the blood of Christ, who through the eternal Spirit offered Himself without spot to God, cleanse your conscience from dead works to serve the living God? (NKJV)

Hebrews 9:26 He then would have had to suffer often since the foundation of the world; but now, once at the end of the ages, He has appeared to put away sin by the sacrifice of Himself. (NKJV)

Hebrews 10:10-12 By that will we have been sanctified through the offering of the body of Jesus Christ once for all. And every priest stands ministering daily and offering repeatedly the same sacrifices, which can never take away sins. But this Man, after He had offered one sacrifice for sins forever, sat down at the right hand of God, (NKJV)

1 John 3:11 For this is the message that you heard from the beginning, that we should love one another, (NKJV)

1 John 3:16) By this we know love, because He laid down His life for us. And we also ought to lay down our lives for the brethren. (NKJV)

1 John 3:23 And this is His commandment: that we should believe on the name of His Son Jesus Christ and love one another, as He gave us commandment. (NKJV)

1 John 4:21And this commandment we have from Him: that he who loves God must love his brother also. (NKJV)

Ephesian 5:3 ¶ But <kai> *fornication, <porneia>* and <de> all <pas> *uncleanness, <akatharsia>* or <e> *covetousness, <pleonexia>* let it <onomazo> not be once <mede> *named <onomazo>* among <en> you, <humin> as <kathos> *becometh <prepo> saints; <hagios>* (KJV)

3 ¶ But fornication and all uncleanness or covetousness, let it not even be named among you, as is fitting for saints; (NKJV)

Key words

Fornication, porneia; harlotry (including adultery and incest); figuratively, idolatry:--fornication.

Uncleanness, akatharsia; impurity (the quality), physically or morally:--uncleanness.

Covetousness, pleonexia; avarice, i.e. (by implication) fraudulency, extortion:--covetous(-ness) practices, greediness.

Named, onomazo; to name, i.e. assign an appellation; by extension, to utter, mention, profess:--call, name.

Becometh, prepo; apparently a primary verb; to tower up (be conspicuous), i.e. (by implication) to be suitable or proper (third person singular present indicative, often used impersonally, it is fit or right):--become, comely.

Saints, hagios; from hagos (an awful thing); sacred (physically, pure, morally blameless or religious, ceremonially, consecrated):--(most) holy (one, thing), saint.

Romans 6:13 And do not present your members as instruments of unrighteousness to sin, but present yourselves to God as being alive from the dead, and your members as instruments of righteousness to God. (NKJV)

1 Corinthians 5:1 It is actually reported that there is sexual immorality among you, and such sexual immorality as is not even named among the Gentiles-- that a man has his father's wife! (NKJV)

1 Corinthians 6:18 Flee sexual immorality. Every sin that a man does is outside the body, but he who commits sexual immorality sins against his own body. (NKJV)

2 Corinthians 12:21 lest, when I come again, my God will humble me among you, and I shall mourn for many who have sinned before and have not repented of the uncleanness, fornication, and lewdness which they have practiced. (NKJV)

Ephesians 4:19-20 Who being past feeling have given themselves over unto lasciviousness, to work all uncleanness with greediness. But ye have not so learned Christ; (KJV)

Colossians 3:5 Mortify therefore your members which are upon the earth; fornication, uncleanness, inordinate affection, evil concupiscence, and covetousness, which is idolatry: (KJV)

1 Thessalonians 4:3 For this is the will of God, even your sanctification, that ye should abstain from fornication: (KJV)

Ephesian 5:4 Neither <kai> *filthiness, <aischrotes>* nor <kai> *foolish talking, <morologia>* nor <e> *jesting, <eutrapelia>* which <ho> are <aneko> not <ou> *convenient: <aneko>* but <alla> rather <mallon> *giving of thanks. <eucharistia>* (KJV)

4 neither filthiness, nor foolish talking, nor coarse jesting, which are not fitting, but rather giving of thanks. (NKJV)

Key words

Filthiness, aischrotes; shamefulness, i.e. obscenity:-- filthiness.

Foolish talking, morologia; silly talk, i.e. buffoonery:-- foolish talking.

Jesting, eutrapelia; (meaning well-turned, i.e. ready at repartee, jocose); witticism, i.e. (in a vulgar sense) ribaldry:--jesting.

Convenient, aneko; to attain to, i.e. (figuratively) be proper:--convenient, be fit.

Giving of thanks, eucharistia; gratitude; actively, grateful language (to God, as an act of worship):-- thankfulness, (giving of) thanks(-giving).

Matthew 12:35 "A good man out of the good treasure of his heart brings forth good things, and an evil man out of the evil treasure brings forth evil things. (NKJV)

Romans 1:28 And even as they did not like to retain God in their knowledge, God gave them over to a debased mind, to do those things which are not fitting; (NKJV)

Ephesians 4:29 Let no corrupt word proceed out of your mouth, but what is good for necessary edification, that it may impart grace to the hearers. (NKJV)

Ephesian 5:5 For <gar> this <touto> ye **know <este>,** **<ginosko>** that <hoti> no <ou> <pas> **whoremonger,** **<pornos>** nor <e> **unclean person, <akathartos>** nor <e> **covetous man, <pleonektes>** who <hos> is <esti> an **idolater, <eidololatres>** hath <echo> any **inheritance** **<kleronomia>** in <en> the kingdom <basileia> of Christ <

5 For this you know, that no fornicator, unclean person, nor covetous man, who is an idolater, has any inheritance in the kingdom of Christ and God. (NKJV)

Key words

Know, este, ginosko; a prolonged form of a primary verb; to "know" (absolutely) in a great variety of applications and with many implications (as follow, with others not thus clearly expressed):--allow, be aware (of), feel, (have) know(-ledge), perceived, be resolved, can speak, be sure, understand.

Whoremonger, pornos; from pernemi (to sell; a (male) prostitute (as venal), i.e. (by analogy) a debauchee (libertine):--fornicator, whoremonger.

Unclean person, akathartos; impure (ceremonially, morally (lewd) or specially, (demonic)):--foul, unclean.

Covetous man, pleonektes; holding (desiring) more, i.e. eager for gain (avaricious, hence a defrauder):--covetous.

Idolater, eidololatres; an image- (servant or) worshipper (literally or figuratively):--idolater.

Inheritance, kleronomia; heirship, i.e. (concretely) a patrimony or (genitive case) a possession:--inheritance.

1 Corinthians 6:9-10 Do you not know that the unrighteous will not inherit the kingdom of God? Do not be deceived. Neither fornicators, nor idolaters, nor adulterers, nor homosexuals, nor sodomites, nor thieves, nor covetous, nor drunkards, nor revilers, nor extortioners will inherit the kingdom of God. (NKJV)

Galatians 5:19-21 Now the works of the flesh are evident, which are: adultery, fornication, uncleanness, lewdness, idolatry, sorcery, hatred, contentions, jealousies, outbursts of wrath, selfish ambitions, dissensions, heresies, envy, murders, drunkenness, revelries, and the like; of which I tell you beforehand, just as I also told you in time past, that those who practice such things will not inherit the kingdom of God. (NKJV)

Colossians 3:5 Therefore put to death your members which are on the earth: fornication, uncleanness, passion, evil desire, and covetousness, which is idolatry. (NKJV)

1 Timothy 6:17 Command those who are rich in this present age not to be haughty, nor to trust in uncertain riches but in the living God, who gives us richly all things to enjoy. (NKJV)

Revelation 22:15 But outside are dogs and sorcerers and sexually immoral and murderers and idolaters, and whoever loves and practices a lie. (NKJV)

Ephesian 5:6 *Let <apatao>* no man <medeis> *deceive <apatao>* you <humas> with *vain <kenos>* words: <logos> for <gar> because <dia> of these things <tauta>

cometh *<erchomai>* the **wrath** *<orge>* of God <theos> upon <epi> the **children** *<huios>* of **disobedience.** *<apeitheia>* {disobedience: or, unbelief} (KJV)

6 Let no one deceive you with empty words, for because of these things the wrath of God comes upon the sons of disobedience. (NKJV)

Key words

Let, deceive, apatao; of uncertain derivation; to cheat, i.e. delude:--deceive.

Vain, kenos; apparently a primary word; empty (literally or figuratively):--empty, (in) vain.

Cometh, erchomai; middle voice of a primary verb (used only in the present and imperfect tenses, the others being supplied by a kindred (middle voice) eleuthomai el-yoo'-thom-ahee, or (active) eltho el'-tho, which do not otherwise occur) to come or go (in a great variety of applications, literally and figuratively):--accompany, appear, bring, come, enter, fall out, go, grow, X light, X next, pass, resort, be set.

Wrath, orge; properly, desire (as a reaching forth or excitement of the mind), i.e. (by analogy), violent passion (ire, or (justifiable) abhorrence); by implication punishment:--anger, indignation, vengeance, wrath.

Children, huios; apparently a primary word; a "son" (sometimes of animals), used very widely of immediate, remote or figuratively, kinship:--child, foal, son.

Disobedience, apeitheia; disbelief (obstinate and rebellious):--disobedience, unbelief.

Jeremiah 29:8 For thus says the LORD of hosts, the God of Israel: Do not let your prophets and your diviners who are in your midst deceive you, nor listen to your dreams which you cause to be dreamed. (NKJV)

Matthew 24:4 And Jesus answered and said to them: "Take heed that no one deceives you. (NKJV)

Romans 1:18 For the wrath of God is revealed from heaven against all ungodliness and unrighteousness of men, who suppress the truth in unrighteousness, (NKJV)

Ephesians 2:2 in which you once walked according to the course of this world, according to the prince of the power of the air, the spirit who now works in the sons of disobedience, (NKJV)

Colossians 2:4 Now this I say lest anyone should deceive you with persuasive words. (NKJV)

Colossians 2:8 Beware lest anyone cheat you through philosophy and empty deceit, according to the tradition of men, according to the basic principles of the world, and not according to Christ. (NKJV)

Colossians 2:18 Let no one cheat you of your reward, taking delight in false humility and worship of angels, intruding into those things which he has not seen, vainly puffed up by his fleshly mind, (NKJV)

Colossians 3:6 Because of these things the wrath of God is coming upon the sons of disobedience, (NKJV)

2 Thessalonians 2:3 Let no one deceive you by any means; for that Day will not come unless the falling away comes first, and the man of sin is revealed, the son of perdition, (NKJV)

Ephesian 5:7 Be <ginomai> not <me> ye <ginomai> therefore <oun> **partakers <summetochos>** with them. <autos> (KJV)

7 Therefore do not be partakers with them. (NKJV)

Key word

Partakers, summetochos; a co-participant:--partaker.

Job 34:8 Who goes in company with the workers of iniquity, And walks with wicked men? (NKJV)

Psalms 50:18 When you saw a thief, you consented with him, And have been a partaker with adulterers. (NKJV)

Numbers 16:26 And he spoke to the congregation, saying, "Depart now from the tents of these wicked men! Touch nothing of theirs, lest you be consumed in all their sins." (NKJV)

Proverbs 1:10-17 My son, if sinners entice you, Do not consent. If they say, "Come with us, Let us lie in wait to shed blood; Let us lurk secretly for the innocent without cause; Let us swallow them alive like Sheol, And whole, like those who go down to the Pit; We shall find all kinds of precious possessions, We shall fill our houses with spoil; Cast in your lot among us, Let us all have one purse" - My son, do not walk in the way with them, Keep your foot from their path; For their feet run to evil, And they make haste to shed blood. Surely, in vain the net is spread In the sight of any bird; (NKJV)

Proverbs 9:6 Forsake foolishness and live, And go in the way of understanding. (NKJV)

Proverbs 13:20) He who walks with wise men will be wise, But the companion of fools will be destroyed. (NKJV)

1 Timothy 5:22 Do not lay hands on anyone hastily, nor share in other people's sins; keep yourself pure. (NKJV)

Revelation 18:4 And I heard another voice from heaven saying, "Come out of her, my people, lest you share in her sins, and lest you receive of her plagues. (NKJV)

Walk in light
Ephesians 5:8-14

Ephesian 5:8 For <gar> ye were <en> sometimes <pote> *darkness, <skotos>* but <de> now <nun> are ye *light <phos>* in <en> the Lord: <kurios> *walk <peripateo>* as <hos> *children <teknon>* of light: <phos> (KJV)

8 For you were once darkness, but now you are light in the Lord. Walk as children of light (NKJV)

Key words

Darkness, skotos; shadiness, i.e. obscurity (literally or figuratively)

Light, phos; from an obsolete phao (to shine or make manifest, especially by rays); luminousness (in the widest application, natural or artificial, abstract or concrete, literal or figurative):--fire, light.

Walk, peripateo; to tread all around, i.e. walk at large (especially as proof of ability); figuratively, to live, deport oneself, follow (as a companion or votary):--go, be occupied with, walk (about).

Children, teknon; a child (as produced):--child, daughter, son.

Isaiah 9:2 The people that walked in darkness have seen a great light: they that dwell in the land of the shadow of death, upon them hath the light shined. (KJV)

Matthew 4:16 The people who sat in darkness have seen a great light, And upon those who sat in the *region and shadow* of death Light has dawned." (NKJV)

Luke 16:8 "So the master commended the unjust steward because he had dealt shrewdly. For the sons of this world are more shrewd in their generation than the sons of light. (NKJV)

Joh 8:12 (John 8:12) Then Jesus spoke to them again, saying, "I am the light of the world. He who follows Me shall not walk in darkness, but have the light of life." (NKJV)

John 12:36 "While you have the light, believe in the light, that you may become sons of light." These things Jesus spoke, and departed, and was hidden from them. (NKJV)

John 12:46 "I have come as a light into the world, that whoever believes in Me should not abide in darkness. (NKJV)

Acts 26:18 'to open their eyes, in order to turn them from darkness to light, and from the power of Satan to God, that they may receive forgiveness of sins and an inheritance among those who are sanctified by faith in Me.' (NKJV)

Romans 1:21 because, although they knew God, they did not glorify Him as God, nor were thankful, but became futile in their thoughts, and their foolish hearts were darkened. (NKJV)

2 Corinthians 3:18 But we all, with unveiled face, beholding as in a mirror the glory of the Lord, are being transformed into the same image from glory to glory, just as by the Spirit of the Lord. (NKJV)

2 Corinthians 4:6 For it is the God who commanded light to shine out of darkness, who has shone in our hearts to give the light of the knowledge of the glory of God in the face of Jesus Christ. (NKJV)

Ephesians 2:11-12 Therefore remember that you, once Gentiles in the flesh--who are called Uncircumcision by what is called the Circumcision made in the flesh by hands-- that at that time you were without Christ, being aliens from the commonwealth of Israel and strangers from the covenants of promise, having no hope and without God in the world. (NKJV)

Ephesians 4:18 having their understanding darkened, being alienated from the life of God, because of the ignorance that is in them, because of the blindness of their heart; (NKJV)

1 Thessalonians 5:5 You are all sons of light and sons of the day. *We are not of the night nor of darkness*. (NKJV)

Titus 3:3 For we ourselves were also once foolish, disobedient, deceived, serving various lusts and pleasures, living in malice and envy, hateful and hating one another. (NKJV)

1 Peter 2:9 But you are a chosen generation, a royal priesthood, a holy nation, His own special people, that you may proclaim the praises of Him who called you out of darkness into His marvelous light; (NKJV)

1 John 2:9 He who says he is in the light, and hates his brother, is in darkness until now. (NKJV)

Ephesian 5:9 (For <gar> the *fruit <karpos>* of the Spirit <pneuma> is in <en> all <pas> *goodness <agathosune>*

and <kai> *righteousness <dikaiosune>* and <kai> *truth; <aletheia>*) (KJV)

9 (for the fruit of the Spirit is in all goodness, righteousness, and truth), (NKJV)

Key words

Fruit, karpos; fruit (as plucked), literally or figuratively:-- fruit.

Goodness, agathosune; virtue or beneficence:-- goodness.

Righteousness, dikaiosune; equity (of character or act); specially (Christian) justification:--righteousness.

Truth, aletheia; true, X truly, truth, verity.

Galatians 5:22 But the fruit of the Spirit is love, joy, peace, longsuffering, kindness, goodness, faithfulness, (NKJV)

Ephesian 5:10 *Proving <dokimazo>* what <tis> is <esti> *acceptable <euarestos>*

unto the Lord. <kurios> (KJV)

10 finding out what is acceptable to the Lord. (NKJV)

Key words

Proving, dokimazo; to test (literally or figuratively); by implication, to approve:--allow, discern, examine, X like, (ap-)prove, try.

Acceptable, euarestos; fully agreeable:--acceptable(-ted), wellpleasing.

Romans 12:2 And do not be conformed to this world, but be transformed by the renewing of your mind, that you may prove what is that good and acceptable and perfect will of God. (NKJV)

Philippians 1:10 that you may approve the things that are excellent, that you may be sincere and without offense till the day of Christ, (NKJV)

1 Thessalonians 5:21 Test all things; hold fast what is good. (NKJV)

1 Timothy 2:3 For this is good and acceptable in the sight of God our Savior, (NKJV)

Ephesian 5:11 And <kai> have <sugkoinoneo> no <me> *fellowship <sugkoinoneo>* with the *unfruitful <akarpos>* *works <ergon>* of *darkness, <skotos>* but <de> rather <mallon> <kai> *reprove <elegcho>* them. (KJV)

11 And have no fellowship with the unfruitful works of darkness, but rather expose them. (NKJV)

Key words

Fellowship, sugkoinoneo; to share in company with, i.e. co-participate in:--communicate (have fellowship) with, be partaker of.

Unfruitful, akarpos; barren (literally or figuratively):-- without fruit, unfruitful.

Works, ergon; from a primary (but obsolete) ergo (to work); toil (as an effort or occupation); by implication, an act:--deed, doing, labour, work.

Darkness, skotos; shadiness, i.e. obscurity (literally or figuratively):--darkness.

Reprove, elegcho; of uncertain affinity; to confute, admonish:--convict, convince, tell a fault, rebuke, reprove.

Leviticus 19:17 'You shall not hate your brother in your heart. You shall surely rebuke your neighbor, and not bear sin because of him. (NKJV)

Romans 6:21 What fruit did you have then in the things of which you are now ashamed? For the end of those things is death. (NKJV)

Romans 13:12The night is far spent, the day is at hand. Therefore let us cast off the works of darkness, and let us put on the armor of light. (NKJV)

1 Corinthians 5:9-11 I wrote to you in my epistle not to keep company with sexually immoral people. Yet I certainly did not mean with the sexually immoral people of this world, or with the covetous, or extortioners, or idolaters, since then you would need to go out of the world. But now I have written to you not to keep company with anyone named a brother, who is sexually immoral, or covetous, or an idolater, or a reviler, or a drunkard, or an extortioner--not even to eat with such a person. (NKJV)

1 Corinthians 10:20 Rather, that the things which the Gentiles sacrifice they sacrifice to demons and not to God, and I do not want you to have fellowship with demons. (NKJV)

2 Corinthians 6:14 Do not be unequally yoked together with unbelievers. For what fellowship has righteousness with lawlessness? And what communion has light with darkness? (NKJV)

Galatians 6:8 For he who sows to his flesh will of the flesh reap corruption, but he who sows to the Spirit will of the Spirit reap everlasting life. (NKJV)

2 Thessalonians 3:6 But we command you, brethren, in the name of our Lord Jesus Christ, that you withdraw from every brother who walks disorderly and not according to the tradition which he received from us. (NKJV)

2 Thessalonians 3:14 And if anyone does not obey our word in this epistle, note that person and do not keep company with him, that he may be ashamed. (NKJV)

1 Timothy 5:20 Those who are sinning rebuke in the presence of all, that the rest also may fear. (NKJV)

Ephesian 5:12 For <gar> it is <esti> a **shame <aischron>** even <kai> to **speak <lego>** of those **things <kruphe>** which are **done <ginomai>** of <hupo> them <autos> in **secret. <kruphe>** (KJV)

12 For it is shameful even to speak of those things which are done by them in secret. (NKJV)

Key words

Shame, aischron; a shameful thing, i.e. indecorum:-- shame.

Speak, lego; a primary verb; properly, to "lay" forth, i.e. (figuratively) relate (in words (usually of systematic or set discourse by implication, to mean:--ask, bid, boast, call, describe, give out, name, put forth, say(-ing, on), shew, speak, tell, utter.

Things, secret. Kruphe; privately:--in secret.

Done, ginomai; a prolongation and middle voice form of a primary verb; to cause to be ("gen"-erate), i.e. (reflexively) to become (come into being), used with great latitude (literal, figurative, intensive, etc.):--arise, be assembled, be(-come, -fall, -have self), be brought (to pass), (be) come (to pass), continue, be divided, draw, be ended, fall, be finished, follow, be found, be fulfilled, + God forbid, grow, happen, have, be kept, be made, be married, be ordained to be, partake, pass, be performed, be published, require, seem, be showed, X soon as it was, sound, be taken, be turned, use, wax, will, would, be wrought.

Romans 1:24-26 Therefore God also gave them up to uncleanness, in the lusts of their hearts, to dishonor their bodies among themselves, who exchanged the truth of God for the lie, and worshiped and served the creature rather than the Creator, who is blessed forever. Amen. For this reason God gave them up to vile passions. For even their women exchanged the natural use for what is against nature. (NKJV)

Ephesian 5:13 But <de> all things <pas> that are *reproved <elegcho>* are made *manifest <phaneroo>* by <hupo> the light: <phos> for <gar> whatsoever <pas> doth make manifest <phaneroo> is <esti> *light. <phos>* {reproved: or, discovered} (KJV)

13 But all things that are exposed are made manifest by the light, for whatever makes manifest is light. (NKJV)

Key words

Reproved, elegcho; of uncertain affinity; to confute, admonish:--convict, convince, tell a fault, rebuke, reprove.

Manifest, phaneroo; to render apparent (literally or figuratively):--appear, manifestly declare, (make) manifest (forth), shew (self).

Light, phos; from an obsolete phao (to shine or make manifest, especially by rays; luminousness (in the widest application, natural or artificial, abstract or concrete, literal or figurative):--fire, light.

John 3:20-21 "For everyone practicing evil hates the light and does not come to the light, lest his deeds should be exposed. "But he who does the truth comes to the light, that his deeds may be clearly seen, that they have been done in God." (NKJV)

Hebrews 4:13 And there is no creature hidden from His sight, but all things are naked and open to the eyes of Him to whom we must give account. (NKJV)

Ephesian 5:14 Wherefore <dio> he saith, <lego> **Awake thou <egeiro>** that **sleepest, <katheudo>** and <kai> **arise <anistemi>** from <ek> the **dead, <nekros>** and <kai> Christ <Christos> shall give <epiphausko> thee <soi> **light. <epiphausko>** {he: or, it} (KJV)

14 Therefore He says: "Awake, you who sleep, Arise from the dead, And Christ will give you light." (NKJV)

Key words

Awake thou, egeiro; (through the idea of collecting one's faculties); to waken (transitively or intransitively), i.e. rouse (literally, from sleep, from sitting or lying, from disease, from death; or figuratively, from obscurity, inactivity, ruins, nonexistence):--awake, lift (up), raise (again, up), rear up, (a-)rise (again, up), stand, take up.

Sleepest, katheudo; (to sleep); to lie down to rest, i.e. (by implication) to fall asleep (literally or figuratively):-- (be a-)sleep.

Arise, anistemi; to stand up (literal or figurative, transitive or intransitive):--arise, lift up, raise up (again), rise (again), stand up(-right).

Dead, nekros; from an apparently primary nekus (a corpse); dead (literally or figuratively; also as noun):-- dead.

Light, epiphausko;   to illuminate (figuratively):--give light.

Isaiah 60:1 Arise, shine; For your light has come! And the glory of the LORD is risen upon you. (NKJV)

John 5:25 "Most assuredly, I say to you, the hour is coming, and now is, when the dead will hear the voice of the Son of God; and those who hear will live. (NKJV)

Romans 6:4-5 Therefore we were buried with Him through baptism into death, that just as **Christ was raised from the dead by the glory of the Father**, even so we also should walk in newness of life. For if we have been united together in the likeness of His death, certainly we also shall be in the likeness of His resurrection, (NKJV)

Romans 13:11-12 And do this, knowing the time, that **now it is high time to awake out of sleep**; for now our salvation is nearer than when we first believed. The night is far spent, the day is at hand. Therefore let us cast off the works of darkness, and let us put on the armor of light. (NKJV)

1 Corinthians 15:34 **Awake to righteousness**, and do not sin; for some do not have the knowledge of God. I speak this to your shame. (NKJV)

Ephesians 2:5 even **when we were dead in trespasses, made us alive together with Christ** (by grace you have been saved) (NKJV)

Colossians 3:1 **If then you were raised with Christ**, seek those things which are above, where Christ is, sitting at the right hand of God. (NKJV)

1 Thessalonians 5:6 **Therefore let us not sleep, as others do**, but let us watch and be sober. (NKJV)

Walk in wisdom

Ephesians 5:15-21

Eph 5:15 **See <blepo>** then <oun> that <pos> ye **walk <peripateo> circumspectly, <akribos>** not <me> as <hos> **fools, <asophos>** but <alla> as <hos> **wise, <sophos>** (KJV)

15 See then that you walk circumspectly, not as fools but as wise, (NKJV)

Key words

See, blepo; a primary verb; to look at (literally or figuratively):--behold, beware, lie, look (on, to), perceive, regard, see, sight, take heed

Walk, peripateo; to tread all around, i.e. walk at large (epecially as proof of ability); figuratively, to live, deport oneself, follow (as a companion or votary):--go, be occupied with, walk (about).

Circumspectly, akribos; exactly:--circumspectly, diligently, perfect(-ly).

Fools, asophos; unwise:--fool.

Wise, sophos; akin to saphes (clear); wise (in a most general application):--wise

Colossians 4:5 Walk in wisdom toward those who are outside, redeeming the time. (NKJV)

Ephesian 5:16 **Redeeming <exagorazo>** the **time, <kairos>** because <hoti> the days <hemera> are <eisi> **evil. <poneros>** (KJV)

16 redeeming the time, because the days are evil. (NKJV)

Key words

Redeeming, exagorazo; to buy up, i.e. ransom; figuratively, to rescue from loss (improve opportunity):-- redeem.

Time, kairos; of uncertain affinity; an occasion, i.e. set or proper time:--X always, opportunity, (convenient, due) season, (due, short, while) time, a while.

Evil, poneros; hurtful, i.e. evil (properly, in effect or influence, figuratively, calamitous; also (passively) ill, i.e. diseased; but especially (morally) culpable, i.e. derelict, vicious, facinorous; neuter (singular) mischief, malice, or (plural) guilt; masculine (singular) the devil, or (plural) sinners:--bad, evil, grievous, harm, lewd, malicious, wicked(-ness).

Ecclesiastes 11:2 Give a portion to seven, and also to eight; for thou knowest not what evil shall be upon the earth. (KJV)

Ecclesiastes 12:1 Remember now thy Creator in the days of thy youth, while the evil days come not, nor the years draw nigh, when thou shalt say, I have no pleasure in them; (KJV)

John 12:35 Then Jesus said unto them, Yet a little while is the light with you. Walk while ye have the light, lest darkness come upon you: for he that walketh in darkness knoweth not whither he goeth. (KJV)

Galatians 6:10 Therefore, as we have opportunity, let us do good to all, especially to those who are of the household of faith. (NKJV)

Ephesians 6:13 Therefore take up the whole armor of God, that you may be able to withstand in the evil day, and having done all, to stand. (NKJV)

Colossians 4:5 Walk in wisdom toward those who are outside, redeeming the time. (NKJV)

Ephesian 5:17 Wherefore <dia> <touto> be ye <ginomai> not <me> **unwise, <aphron>** but <alla> **understanding <suniemi>** what <tis> the **will <thelema>** of the Lord <kurios> is. (KJV)

17 Therefore do not be unwise, but understand what the will of the Lord is. (NKJV)

Key words

Unwise, aphron; properly, mindless, i.e. stupid, (by implication) ignorant, (specially) egotistic, (practically) rash, or (morally) unbelieving:--fool(-ish), unwise.

Understanding, suniemi; to put together, i.e. (mentally) to comprehend; by implication, to act piously:-- consider, understand, be wise.

Will, thelema; a determination (properly, the thing), i.e. (actively) choice (specially, purpose, decree; abstractly, volition) or (passively) inclination:-- desire, pleasure, will.

Ro 12:2 (Romans 12:2) And do not be conformed to this world, but be transformed by the renewing of your mind, that you may prove what is that good and acceptable and perfect will of God. (NKJV)

Colossians 4:5 Walk in wisdom toward those who are outside, redeeming the time. (NKJV)

1 Thessalonians 4:3 For this is the will of God, your sanctification: that you should abstain from sexual immorality; (NKJV)

1 Thessalonians 5:18 in everything give thanks; for this is the will of God in Christ Jesus for you. (NKJV)

Ephesian 5:18 And <kai> be <methusko> not <me> *drunk <methusko>* with *wine, <oinos>* wherein <en> <hos> is <esti> *excess; <asotia>* but <alla> be *filled <pleroo>* with <en> the Spirit; <pneuma> (KJV)

18 And do not be drunk with wine, in which is dissipation; but be filled with the Spirit, (NKJV)

Key words

Drunk, methusko; to intoxicate:--be drunk(-en).

Wine, oinos; a primary word (or perhaps of Hebrew origin); "wine" (literally or figuratively):--wine.

Excess, asotia; properly, unsavedness, i.e. (by implication) profligacy:--excess, riot.

Filled, pleroo; to make replete, i.e. (literally) to cram (a net), level up (a hollow), or (figuratively) to furnish (or imbue, diffuse, influence), satisfy, execute (an office), finish (a period or task), verify (or coincide with a prediction), etc.:--accomplish, X after, (be) complete, end, expire, fill (up), fulfil, (be, make) full (come), fully preach, perfect, supply.

Proverbs 20:1 Wine is a mocker, Strong drink is a brawler, And whoever is led astray by it is not wise. (NKJV)

Proverbs 23:20 Do not mix with winebibbers, Or with gluttonous eaters of meat; (NKJV)

Proverbs 23:30 Those who linger long at the wine, Those who go in search of mixed wine. (NKJV)

Isaiah 5:11 Woe to those who rise early in the morning, That they may follow intoxicating drink; Who continue until night, till wine inflames them! (NKJV)

Isaiah 5:22 Woe to men mighty at drinking wine, Woe to men valiant for mixing intoxicating drink, (NKJV)

Luke 21:34 "But take heed to yourselves, lest your hearts be weighed down with carousing, drunkenness, and cares of this life, and that Day come on you unexpectedly. (NKJV)

Ephesian 5:19 *Speaking* *<laleo>* to yourselves <heautou> in *psalms* *<psalmos>* and <kai> *hymns* *<humnos>* and <kai> *spiritual* *<pneumatikos>* *songs,* *<ode>* *singing* *<ado>* and <kai> *making melody* *<psallo>* in <en> your <humon> *heart* *<kardia>* to the Lord; <kurios> (KJV)

19 speaking to one another in psalms and hymns and spiritual songs, singing and making melody in your heart to the Lord, (NKJV)

Key words

Speaking, laleo; a prolonged form of an otherwise obsolete verb; to talk, i.e. utter words:--preach, say, speak (after), talk, tell, utter

Psalms, psalmos; a set piece of music, i.e. a sacred ode (accompanied with the voice, harp or other instrument; a "psalm"); collectively, the book of the Psalms:--psalm.

Hymns, humnos; apparently from a simpler (obsolete) form of hudeo (to celebrate; a "hymn" or religious ode (one of the Psalms):--hymn.

Spiritual, pneumatikos; non-carnal, i.e. (humanly) ethereal (as opposed to gross), or (daemoniacally) a spirit (concretely), or (divinely) supernatural, regenerate, religious:--spiritual.

Songs, ode; a chant or "ode" (the general term for any words sung

Singing ado; to sing:--sing.

Making melody, psallo; probably strengthened from psao (to rub or touch the surface; to twitch or twang, i.e. to play on a stringed instrument (celebrate the divine worship with music and accompanying odes):--make melody, sing (psalms).

Heart, kardia; prolonged from a primary kar (Latin cor, "heart"); the heart, i.e. (figuratively) the thoughts or feelings (mind); also (by analogy) the middle:--(+ broken-)heart(-ed).

Acts 16:25 But at midnight Paul and Silas were praying and singing hymns to God, and the prisoners were listening to them. (NKJV)

1 Corinthians 14:26 How is it then, brethren? Whenever you come together, each of you has a psalm, has a teaching, has a tongue, has a revelation, has an interpretation. Let all things be done for edification. (NKJV)

Colossians 3:16 Let the word of Christ dwell in you richly in all wisdom, teaching and admonishing one another in psalms and hymns and spiritual songs, singing with grace in your hearts to the Lord. (NKJV)

James 5:13 Is anyone among you suffering? Let him pray. Is anyone cheerful? Let him sing psalms. (NKJV)

Ephesian 5:20 **Giving thanks <eucharisteo>** always <pantote> for <huper> all things <pas> unto God <theos> and <kai> the Father <pater> in <en> the **name <onoma>** of our <hemon> Lord <kurios> Jesus <Iesous> Christ; <Christos> (KJV)

20 giving thanks always for all things to God the Father in the name of our Lord Jesus Christ, (NKJV)

Key words

Giving thanks, eucharisteo; to be grateful, i.e. (actively) to express gratitude (towards); specially, to say grace at a meal:--(give) thank(-ful, -s).

Name, onoma; a "name" (literally or figuratively) (authority, character):--called, (+ sur-)name(-d).

Psalms 34:1 <<A Psalm of David, when he changed his behaviour before Abimelech; who drove him away, and he departed.>> **I will bless the LORD at all times**: his **praise shall continually** be in my mouth. {Abimelech: or, Achish} (KJV)

Isaiah 63:7 I will mention the lovingkindnesses of the LORD, and the praises of the LORD, according to all that the LORD hath bestowed on us, and the great goodness toward the house of Israel, which he hath bestowed on them according to his mercies, and according to the multitude of his lovingkindnesses. (KJV)

Colossians 3:17 And *whatever you do in word or deed*, do all in the name of the Lord Jesus, **giving thanks** to God the Father through Him. (NKJV)

1 Thessalonians 5:18 **in everything give thanks**; for this is the will of God in Christ Jesus for you. (NKJV)

2 Thessalonians 1:3 We are bound to thank God always for you, brethren, as it is fitting, because your faith grows exceedingly, and the love of every one of you all abounds toward each other, (NKJV)

Hebrews 13:15 Therefore by Him **let us continually offer the sacrifice of praise to God**, that is, the fruit of our lips, giving thanks to His name. (NKJV)

1 Peter 2:5 you also, as living stones, are being built up a spiritual house, a holy priesthood, **to offer up spiritual sacrifices acceptable to God** through Jesus Christ. (NKJV)

1 Peter 4:11 If anyone speaks, let him speak as the oracles of God. If anyone ministers, let him do it as with the ability which God supplies, **that in all things God may be glorified through Jesus Christ,** to whom belong the glory and the dominion forever and ever. Amen. (NKJV)

Ephesian 5:21 ¶ *Submitting yourselves <hupotasso>* one to another <allelon> in <en> the *fear <phobos>* of God. <theos> (KJV)

21 ¶ submitting to one another in the fear of God. (NKJV)

Key words

Submitting yourselves, hupotasso; to subordinate; reflexively, to obey:--be under obedience (obedient), put under, subdue unto, (be, make) subject (to, unto), be (put) in subjection (to, under), submit self unto.

Fear, phobos; from a primary phebomai (to be put in fear); alarm or fright:--be afraid, + exceedingly, fear, terror.

Philippians 2:3 Let nothing be done through selfish ambition or conceit, but in lowliness of mind *let each esteem others better than himself*. (NKJV)

1 Peter 5:5 Likewise you younger people, submit yourselves to your elders. *Yes, all of you be submissive to one another, and be clothed with humility*, for "God resists the proud, But gives grace to the humble." (NKJV)

Marriage-Christ and the Church

Ephesians 5:22-33

Ephesian 5:22 ***Wives, <gune> submit yourselves <hupotasso>*** unto your ***own <idios> husbands, <aner>*** as <hos> unto the Lord. <kurios> (KJV)

22 Wives, submit to your own husbands, as to the Lord. (NKJV)

Key words

Wives, gune; a woman; specially, a wife:--wife, woman.

Submit yourselves, hupotasso; to subordinate; reflexively, to obey:--be under obedience (obedient), put under, subdue unto, (be, make) subject (to, unto), be (put) in subjection (to, under), submit self unto.

Own, idios; of uncertain affinity; pertaining to self, i.e. one's own; by implication, private or separate:--X his acquaintance, when they were alone, apart, aside, due, his (own, proper, several), home, (her, our, thine, your) own (business), private(-ly), proper, severally, their (own).

Husbands, aner; a primary word, a man (properly as an individual male):--fellow, husband, man, sir.

Genesis 3:16 To the woman He said: "I will greatly multiply your sorrow and your conception; In pain you shall bring forth children; Your desire shall be for your husband, And he shall rule over you." (NKJV)

1 Corinthians 14:34 Let your women keep silent in the churches, for they are not permitted to speak; but they are to be submissive, as the law also says. (NKJV)

Ephesians 6:5 Bondservants, be obedient to those who are your masters according to the flesh, with fear and trembling, in sincerity of heart, as to Christ; (NKJV)

Colossians 3:18 Wives, submit to your own husbands, as is fitting in the Lord. (NKJV)

Titus 2:5 to be discreet, chaste, homemakers, good, obedient to their own husbands, that the word of God may not be blasphemed. (NKJV)

1 Peter 3:1 Wives, likewise, be submissive to your own husbands, that even if some do not obey the word, they, without a word, may be won by the conduct of their wives, (NKJV)

Ephesian 5:23 For <hoti> the husband <aner> is <esti> the **head <kephale>** of the wife, <gune> even <kai> as <hos> Christ <Christos> is the head <kephale> of the **church: <ekklesia>** and <kai> he <autos> is <esti> the **saviour <soter>** of the **body. <soma>** (KJV)

23 For the husband is head of the wife, as also Christ is head of the church; and He is the Savior of the body. (NKJV)

Key words

Head, kephale; from the primary kapto (in the sense of seizing); the head (as the part most readily taken hold of), literally or figuratively:--head.

Church, ekklesia; a calling out, i.e. (concretely) a popular meeting, especially a religious congregation (Jewish synagogue, or Christian community of members on earth or saints in heaven or both):--assembly, church.

Saviour, soter; a deliverer, i.e. God or Christ:--saviour.

Body, soma; the body (as a sound whole), used in a very wide application, literally or figuratively:--bodily, body, slave.

1 Corinthians 11:3 But I want you to know that the head of every man is Christ, the head of woman is man, and the head of Christ is God. (NKJV)

Ephesians 1:22-23 And He put all things under His feet, and gave Him to be head over all things to the church, which is His body, the fullness of Him who fills all in all. (NKJV)

Ephesians 4:15 but, speaking the truth in love, may grow up in all things into Him who is the head--Christ-- (NKJV)

Colossians 1:18 And He is the head of the body, the church, who is the beginning, the firstborn from the dead, that in all things He may have the preeminence. (NKJV)

Ephesian 5:24 Therefore <alla> as <hosper> the church <ekklesia> is subject <hupotasso> unto Christ, <Christos> so <houto> <kai> let the wives <gune> be to their own <idios> husbands <aner> in <en> *every thing.* *<pas>* (KJV)

24 Therefore, just as the church is subject to Christ, so let the wives be to their own husbands in everything. (NKJV)

Key words

Every thing, pas; including all the forms of declension; apparently a primary word; all, any, every, the whole:-- all (manner of, means), alway(-s), any (one), X daily, + ever, every (one, way), as many as, + no(-thing), X thoroughly, whatsoever, whole, whosoever.

Colossians 3:20-22 Children, obey your parents in all things, for this is well pleasing to the Lord. Fathers, do not provoke your children, lest they become discouraged. Bondservants, obey in all things your masters according to the flesh, not with eyeservice, as men-pleasers, but in sincerity of heart, fearing God. (NKJV)

Tit 2:9 (Titus 2:9) Exhort bondservants to be obedient to their own masters, to be well pleasing in all things, not answering back, (NKJV)

Ephesian 5:25 Husbands, <aner> *love <agapao>* your <heautou> wives, <gune> even as <kathos> Christ <Christos> also <kai> loved <agapao> the church, <ekklesia> and <kai> *gave <paradidomi>* himself <heautou> for <huper> it; <autos> (KJV)

25 Husbands, love your wives, just as Christ also loved the church and gave Himself for her, (NKJV)

Key words

Love, agapao; perhaps from agan (much); to love (in a social or moral sense):--(be-)love(-ed)

Gave, paradidomi; to surrender, i.e yield up, intrust, transmit:--betray, bring forth, cast, commit, deliver (up), give (over, up), hazard, put in prison, recommend.

Acts 20:28 "Therefore take heed to yourselves and to all the flock, among which the Holy Spirit has made you overseers, to shepherd the church of God which He purchased with His own blood. (NKJV)

Galatians 1:4 who gave Himself for our sins, that He might deliver us from this present evil age, according to the will of our God and Father, (NKJV)

Galatians 2:20 "I have been crucified with Christ; it is no longer I who live, but Christ lives in me; and the life which I now live in the flesh I live by faith in the Son of God, who loved me and gave Himself for me. (NKJV)

Ephesians 5:2 And walk in love, as Christ also has loved us and given Himself for us, an offering and a sacrifice to God for a sweet-smelling aroma. (NKJV)

Colossians 3:19 Husbands, love your wives and do not be bitter toward them. (NKJV)

1 Peter 3:7 Husbands, likewise, dwell with them with understanding, giving honor to the wife, as to the weaker vessel, and as being heirs together of the grace of life, that your prayers may not be hindered. (NKJV)

Ephesian 5:26 That <hina> he might *sanctify <hagiazo>* and *cleanse it <katharizo>* with the *washing <loutron>* of water <hudor> by <en> the *word, <rhema>* (KJV)

26 that He might sanctify and cleanse her with the washing of water by the word, (NKJV)

Key words

Sanctify, hagiazo; to make holy, i.e. (ceremonially) purify or consecrate; (mentally) to venerate:--hallow, be holy, sanctify.

Cleanse it, katharizo; to cleanse (literally or figuratively):--(make) clean(-se), purge, purify.

Washing, loutron; a bath, i.e. (figuratively), baptism:--washing.

Word, rhema; an utterance (individually, collectively or specially),; by implication, a matter or topic (especially of narration, command or dispute); with a negative naught whatever:--+ evil, + nothing, saying, word.

John 3:5 Jesus answered, "Most assuredly, I say to you, unless one is born of water and the Spirit, he cannot enter the kingdom of God. (NKJV)

John 15:3 "You are already clean because of the word which I have spoken to you. (NKJV)

John 17:17 "Sanctify them by Your truth. Your word is truth. (NKJV)

Titus 3:5 not by works of righteousness which we have done, but according to His mercy He saved us, through the washing of regeneration and renewing of the Holy Spirit, (NKJV)

Hebrews 10:22 let us draw near with a true heart in full assurance of faith, having our hearts sprinkled from an evil conscience and our bodies washed with pure water. (NKJV)

1 John 5:6 This is He who came by water and blood-- Jesus Christ; not only by water, but by water and blood. And it is the Spirit who bears witness, because the Spirit is truth. (NKJV)

Ephesian 5:27 That <hina> he might **present <paristemi>** it <autos> to himself <heautou> a **glorious <endoxos> church, <ekklesia>** not <me> having <echo> **spot, <spilos>** or <e> **wrinkle, <rhutis>** or <e> any <tis> such thing; <toioutos> but <alla> that <hina> it should be <o> **holy <hagios>** and <kai> **without blemish. <amomos>** (KJV)

27 that He might present her to Himself a glorious church, not having spot or wrinkle or any such thing, but that she should be holy and without blemish. (NKJV)

Key words

Present, paristemi; to stand beside, i.e. (transitively) to exhibit, proffer, (specially), recommend, (figuratively) substantiate; or (intransitively) to be at hand (or ready), aid:--assist, bring before, command, commend, give presently, present, prove, provide, shew, stand (before, by, here, up, with), yield.

Glorious, endoxos; in glory, i.e. splendid, (figuratively) noble:--glorious, gorgeous(-ly), honourable.

Church, ekklesia; a calling out, i.e. (concretely) a popular meeting, especially a religious congregation (Jewish synagogue, or Christian community of members on earth or saints in heaven or both):--assembly, church.

Spot, spilos; of uncertain derivation; a stain or blemish, i.e. (figuratively) defect, disgrace:--spot.

Wrinkle, rhutis; a fold (as drawing together), i.e. a wrinkle (especially on the face):--wrinkle.

Holy, hagios; from hagos (an awful thing); sacred (physically, pure, morally blameless or religious, ceremonially, consecrated):--(most) holy (one, thing), saint.

Without blemish, amomos; unblemished (literally or figuratively):--without blame (blemish, fault, spot), faultless, unblamable.

(Song of Solomon 4:7) You are all fair, my love, And there is no spot in you. (NKJV)

2 Corinthians 11:2 For I am jealous for you with godly jealousy. For I have betrothed you to one husband, that I may present you as a chaste virgin to Christ. (NKJV)

Ephesians 1:4 just as He chose us in Him before the foundation of the world, that we should be holy and without blame before Him in love, (NKJV)

Colossians 1:22 in the body of His flesh through death, to present you holy, and blameless, and above reproach in His sight (NKJV)

Ephesian 5:28 So <houto> ought <opheilo> men <aner> to *love <agapao>* their <heautou> wives <gune> as <hos> their own <heautou> bodies. <soma> He that loveth <agapao> his <heautou> wife <gune> loveth <agapao> himself. <heautou> (KJV)

28 So husbands ought to love their own wives as their own bodies; he who loves his wife loves himself. (NKJV)

Key words

Love, agapao; perhaps from agan (much; to love (in a social or moral sense):--(be-)love(-ed)

Ephesian 5:29 For <gar> no man <oudeis> ever yet <pote> **hated <miseo>** his own <heautou> **flesh; <sarx>** but <alla> **nourisheth <ektrepho>** and <kai> **cherisheth <thalpo>** it, <autos> even as <kathos> <kai> the Lord <kurios> the church: <ekklesia> (KJV)

29 For no one ever hated his own flesh, but nourishes and cherishes it, just as the Lord does the church. (NKJV)

Key words

Hated, m iseo; from a primary misos (hatred); to detest (especially to persecute); by extension, to love less:--hate(-ful).

Flesh, sarx; flesh (as stripped of the skin), i.e. (strictly) the meat of an animal (as food), or (by extension) the body (as opposed to the soul (or spirit), or as the symbol of what is external, or as the means of kindred), or (by implication) human nature (with its frailties (physically or morally) and passions), or (specially), a human being (as such):--carnal(-ly, + -ly minded), flesh(-ly).

Nourisheth, ektrepho; to rear up to maturity, i.e. (genitive case) to cherish or train:--bring up, nourish.

Cherisheth, thalpo; probably akin to thallo (to warm); to brood, i.e. (figuratively) to foster:--cherish.

Ephesian 5:30 For <hoti> we are <esmen> **members <melos>** of his <autos> **body, <soma>** of <ek> his <autos> flesh, <sarx> and <kai> of <ek> his <autos> **bones. <osteon>** (KJV)

30 For we are members of His body, of His flesh and of His bones. (NKJV)

Key words

Members, melos; of uncertain affinity; a limb or part of the body:--member.

Body, soma; the body (as a sound whole), used in a very wide application, literally or figuratively:--bodily, body, slave.

Bones, osteon; of uncertain affinity; a bone:--bone.

Genesis 2:23 And Adam said: "This is now bone of my bones And flesh of my flesh; She shall be called Woman, Because she was taken out of Man." (NKJV)

Romans 12:5 so we, being many, are one body in Christ, and individually members of one another. (NKJV)

1 Corinthians 6:15 Do you not know that your bodies are members of Christ? Shall I then take the members of Christ and make them members of a harlot? Certainly not! (NKJV)

1 Corinthians 12:27 Now you are the body of Christ, and members individually. (NKJV)

Ephesian 5:31 For <anti> this cause <toutou> shall <kataleipo> a man <anthropos> *leave <kataleipo>* his <autos> father <pater> and <kai> mother, <meter> and <kai> shall be *joined <proskollao>* unto <pros> his <autos> wife, <gune> and <kai> they two <duo> shall be <esomai> one <eis> <mia> flesh. <sarx> (KJV)

31 "For this reason a man shall leave his father and mother and be joined to his wife, and the two shall become one flesh." (NKJV)

Key words

Leave, kataleipo; to leave down, i.e. behind; by implication, to abandon, have remaining:--forsake, leave, reserve.

Joined, proskollao; to glue to, i.e. (figuratively) to adhere:--cleave, join (self).

Genesis 2:24 Therefore a man shall leave his father and mother and be joined to his wife, and they shall become one flesh. (NKJV)

Matthew 19:5 "and said, 'For this reason a man shall leave his father and mother and be joined to his wife, and the two shall become one flesh'? (NKJV)

Mark 10:7-8)'For this reason a man shall leave his father and mother and be joined to his wife, 'and the two shall become one flesh'; so then they are no longer two, but one flesh. (NKJV)

1 Corinthians 6:16 Or do you not know that he who is joined to a harlot is one body with her? For "the two," He says, "shall become one flesh." (NKJV)

Ephesian 5:32 This <touto> is <esti> a **great** **<megas>** **mystery:** **<musterion>** but <de> I <ego> speak <lego> concerning <eis> **Christ** **<Christos>** and <eis> <kai> the **church.** **<ekklesia>** (KJV)

32 This is a great mystery, but I speak concerning Christ and the church. (NKJV)

Key words

Great, megas; (including the prolonged forms, feminine megale, plural megaloi, etc.; big (literally or figuratively, in a very wide application):--(+ fear) exceedingly, great(-est), high, large, loud, mighty, + (be) sore (afraid), strong, X to years.

Mystery, musterion; from a derivative of muo (to shut the mouth); a secret or "mystery" (through the idea of silence imposed by initiation into religious rites):--mystery.

Christ, Christos; anointed, i.e. the Messiah, an epithet of Jesus:--Christ.

Church, ekklesia; a calling out, i.e. (concretely) a popular meeting, especially a religious congregation (Jewish synagogue, or Christian community of members on earth or saints in heaven or both):--assembly, church.

Ephesian 5:33 Nevertheless <plen> <kai> let <agapao> every one <heis> <hekastos> of you <humeis> in particular <kata> so <houto> *love <agapao>* his <heautou> wife <gune> even as <hos> himself; <heautou> and <de> the wife <gune> see that <hina> she *reverence <phobeo>* her husband. <aner> (KJV)

33 Nevertheless let each one of you in particular so love his own wife as himself, and let the wife see that she respects her husband. (NKJV)

Key words

Love, agapao; perhaps from agan (much); to love (in a social or moral sense):--(be-)love(-ed

Reverence, phobeo; to frighten, i.e. (passively) to be alarmed; by analogy, *to be in awe of*, i.e. revere:--be (+ sore) afraid, fear (exceedingly), *reverence*.

Colossians 3:19 Husbands, love your wives and do not be bitter toward them. (NKJV)

1 Peter 3:6 as Sarah obeyed Abraham, calling him lord, whose daughters you are if you do good and are not afraid with any terror. (NKJV)

References used in this study

Power Bible CD
Phil Lindner, Online Publishing, Inc
P.O. Box 21
Bronson, MI 49028
PowerBible.com

Thank you for studying God's word with us. I trust that this study guide has been a blessing to you. Additional study guides are available;

Hosea study guide
Sowing and Reaping study guide
Psalms 91 study guide
Psalms 23 study guide
Psalms 1 study guide
Psalms 150 study guide
Psalms 63 study guide
Psalms 100 study guide
Psalm 47 study guide
Psalm 26 study guide
Psalms 93 study guide
Psalms 98 study guide
Prophetic leadership study guide
The Throne of God study guide
Corinthians 10 the price of ministry study guide
Jesus is Better study guide
John 17 study guide
Jude study guide

Ephesians Chapter one (one of six)
Ephesians Chapter two (two of six)
Ephesians Chapter three (three of six)
Ephesians Chapter four (four of six)
Ephesians Chapter five (five of six)
Ephesians Chapter six (six of six)

Amazon.com/author/angelsantiago

.

Angel Perez Ministries
1550 SE 14th Street Apt 28
Lincoln City, Oregon 97367
Email; recoveryyes123@yahoo.com

Seminars

Relapse prevention the bible way
Lay counselors training
Drug free that's me
Weekend in the word

To schedule a seminar please
contact at our office

Missions Projects and opportunities

Sponsor a feeding station $100.00
Sponsor a Pastor $25.00
Sponsor a bag of rice $60.00
Sponsor a feeding bowl $.50 cents
Sponsor a mission's trip
- Flight $1,200.00

Your gift of any size will help us to continue our outreach in the Philippines

Printed in Great Britain
by Amazon

14984187R00046